The Enemies of Salvation

THE ENEMIES OF SALVATION

The Flesh, the World, and the Devil

BISHOP GEORGE HAY

TAN Books
Gastonia, North Carolina

Originally published in *Works of the Right Rev. Bishop Hay Vol. III The Devout Christian: Vol. I* by William Blackwood and Sons in 1871.

Typesetting and revisions in *The Enemies of Salvation: The World, the Flesh, and the Devil* © 2021 TAN Books

Cover design by Caroline Green

Cover image: Resurrection of the dead, demon, detail from the Coronation of the Virgin, 1453-54 (oil on panel), Quarton, Enguerrand (c.1410-66) / French, Bridgeman Images

ISBN: 978-1-5051-2263-3
Kindle ISBN: 978-1-5051-2264-0
ePUB ISBN: 978-1-5051-2265-7

Published in the United States by
TAN Books
PO Box 269
Gastonia, NC 28053
www.TANBooks.com

Printed in the United States of America

The Enemies of Salvation is part of the TAN Books series which includes old, timeless Catholic books that have been updated and now reprinted for your spiritual growth. Besides producing traditional Catholic content from living authors, TAN Books looks to the saints and spiritual masters of the past to guide us in the present and into the future to our true home, heaven. The Enemies of Salvation was written by renowned the Scottish bishop George Hay, who lived from 1729 to 1811.

CONTENTS

A SHORT BIOGRAPHY OF BISHOP GEORGE HAY

"Since the religious revolution of the sixteenth century, to no man has the Catholic Church in Scotland been so much indebted as to Bishop Hay. He is preeminently her bishop of the last three hundred years."

—Bishop John Strain, Archbishop of the Metropolitan see of St. Andrews and Edinburgh, 1810–1883

Bishop George Hay was born into a Protestant family in the year 1729 in Edinburgh. Hay lived during a difficult time in Scotland, and at the age of sixteen, he was forced to join the battle of Prestonpans. The summons to help injured soldiers disrupted his education at Edinburgh University, where he was forging a promising path towards a medical career. Swept up in the politics and fighting of the time, Hay accompanied Charles Edward Stuart's army until he became ill and returned home. Hay, like his father before him, was punished for his support of the Stuarts and was taken into custody in London for twelve months. While information about how religious Hay was up to this point is scarce, he may have been largely influenced by his parent's Episcopalian faith. Interestingly, it was during his time in custody that Hay was first introduced to the teachings of the Catholic faith by a man named Neighan. After serving time in London, he returned to Edinburgh, and the rest of Hay's teenage years were spent learning about the Catholic faith. Hay studied works by Catholic thinkers, including a fellow convert named John Gother. Hay read Gother's work entitled "A Papist Misrepresented and Represented", which outlined a number of misconceptions of Catholic doctrine and his responses to them. Undoubtedly, Hay learned a great deal just from studying on his own, but he soon received instruction from a Jesuit missionary named Father Seaton. As a result, Hay was able to receive his first Communion and enter fully into the Catholic faith at the age of twenty.

The systematic suppression of Catholicism in Scotland during Hay's life was due to the Scottish Reformation that began just under two hundred years before he was born. The strict penal laws that now applied to Hay, a newly practicing Catholic, prohibited him from completing his medical degree. Instead, he boarded a vessel as a surgeon and traversed the Mediterranean Sea. On one of the ship's stops, by divine providence, he met the vicar apostolic of the London District of the time, Bishop Richard Challoner. Through this friendship, Hay became convinced of his mission to become a priest. Hay found his way to Rome, where he studied for roughly eight years at Scots College. Hay was ordained in 1758 by Cardinal Spinelli, about nine years after his reception into the Church. Hay's road to becoming a bishop was due in large part to his assistantship to Bishop Grant, who was located in the Enzie district in Banffshire. Not too long after Bishop Grant accepted Hay as his assistant, he took Bishop Smith's place as Lowland vicar apostolic. In this new position, Bishop Grant was given permission to bring Hay along as his coadjutor. This secured Hay as Bishop Grant's successor, and he was consecrated as coadjutor bishop on Trinity Sunday in the year 1769. Hay's consecration was supposedly done in secret, with a limited attendance due to the penal laws. Shortly afterward, in the year 1778, he officially succeeded Bishop Grant as Lowland vicar apostolic. Thus began Bishop Hay's challenging yet fruitful work of the vicariate during which time he strove tirelessly to unite the Church.

In the nearly thirty-five years Bishop Hay served as bishop of the Lowland District, he published written works, played a major role in Scotland's eventual acceptance of Catholicism, and endeavored to reform seminaries. Bishop Hay is credited for publishing the first English Bible in Scotland, though he is better known for his original work centered on Catholic doctrine. Between 1781 and 1786, Bishop Hay published three successive works entitled *The Sincere Christian*, *The Devout Christian* (reprinted in part here), and *The Pious Christian*. Each of Hay's works, meticulously grounded in Scripture and in Church teaching, reinforce the importance of recognizing the infallible authority of the Church and the necessary unification under the Catholic Church as the true source of salvation. As stated before, Bishop Hay was living through the effects of the Scottish Reformation that began in 1560. Perhaps more than anything else, the people of his time needed to be reminded of the authority of the Church and its role in the salvation of its people.

Within Hay's first year as bishop, a group of rioters burned down his newly constructed chapel and house in Edinburgh in response to his public attempts to bring Catholics out of oppression. In the aftermath of the fire, it was reported that most all of his possessions were either burnt or sold at auction. The government did little in response, which included a small sum in compensation. Through it all, Bishop Hay was widely regarded for his even temperament and did not waver in his determination to help his fellow Catholics. Bishop Hay's tireless efforts to bring relief to the Catholics he served were finally rewarded in 1793 when, from an act of Parliament, most of the penal laws were lifted. What a relief it must have been for Bishop Hay that he could live to see the acceptance of Catholicism in Scotland.

Bishop Hay's work in forming future priests is outlined by his efforts to further develop the seminaries around him. For example, Hay visited the pope in Rome, where he stayed for about six months, in an attempt to receive permission and support to reorganize Scots College, where he also attended seminary. Bishop Hay's main goal was to have Scottish superiors assigned to the college, but it would take a few years for his plans to come to fruition. Bishop Hay also had plans for seminaries in Paris, but the political conflict in France halted is efforts. As part of his last public ministry, Hay also established a new seminary in Aberdeenshire at the Aquhorthies College.

With great patience, Bishop Hay awaited permission to appoint his coadjutor bishop, Dr. Alexander

Cameron, and then was able to retire. Bishop Hay died in his early eighties, in 1811, not long after his retirement. Bishop Hay's devotion to his faith and the souls under his care, in the face of Catholic oppression, is truly admirable. His work as a catalyst for the acceptance of Catholicism in Scotland carried his influence beyond his place and time. The value of Bishop Hay's writings is not lost on today's world. In fact, it is needed in the present as a reminder of the Catholic response to Protestantism and the hope for unification of all people under one faith.

PART 1

ETERNAL SALVATION

1

THE LAST END OF MAN

We shall consider eternal salvation itself, its excellence and importance; that we may see how much it is our only true interest to serve God here, since our eternal happiness, which is our last end, depends upon our so doing.

The end for which God created us is to glorify Him by loving and serving Him; this is the immediate end for which we have our being, for which we are placed in this world. All creatures around us are made for our use, and serve to show the infinite power, wisdom, and goodness of our great Creator, with His other Divine perfections. The wonderful things He has done for us disclose still more fully His sublime excellence, and convince us how much He deserves to be loved, praised, and glorified.

But His design in creating us does not stop here. He made us not for this present life alone, but for eternity.

When this transitory life ends, we begin another which will continue forever. Such is His infinite goodness, that if we faithfully comply with the end of our being, by serving and glorifying Him here, He will hereafter reward us with eternal salvation, which is the possession of incomprehensible happiness, the enjoyment of God Himself for eternity. Therefore salvation is called our last end, as being the end which God had in view with regard to us, in creating us: "You have your fruit unto sanctification, and the end everlasting life" (Rom. 6:22).

The supreme and ultimate end which God had in creating us was His own glory; so that not only in this life are we bound to glorify God as the immediate end of our being, but this also will be the happy employment of the blessed for eternity. Our eternal happiness essentially consists in seeing God, and in loving, enjoying, and glorifying Him forever!

2

OUR HAPPINESS IN SEEING GOD

*If created bodily beauty, which is nothing compared
to the spiritual beauty of the soul, and still less to the
supernatural beauty of a being in glory, has such charms
to please and delight, how much more must the infinite
uncreated beauty of God beatify the souls of the blessed,
filling them with inconceivable rapture and delight?*

On account of His infinite beauty and number-less perfections, our happiness consists in seeing God. We find, from experience, that our nature is so framed by our Creator as to receive particular pleasure and delight from beholding any object which is beautiful and perfect in its kind. Of material beauty, that of the human form is the most excellent, and when this is singularly remarkable, it attracts and enchants the hearts even of the wise; witness the examples of Sampson, Solomon, Holophernes, and others.

Now, if created bodily beauty, which is nothing compared to the spiritual beauty of the soul, and still less to the supernatural beauty of a being in glory, has such charms to please and delight, how much more must the infinite uncreated beauty of God beatify the souls of the blessed, filling them with inconceivable rapture and delight? Our souls and hearts are made for God: no creature is capable of satisfying their boundless capacity; nothing but an infinite good can fill them; nothing but the sight and possession of the beauty of God, the infinite good for which they were created, can give them entire contentment.

This is impossible for us to form any just idea of what the beauty of God is in itself; for how can a finite being form any just idea of what is infinite? How can the creature have any adequate idea of what essentially belongs to the Creator? Besides, we have no grounds to go upon, any more than a blind man has to form a just idea of light and color. The beauty of God is of a kind totally different from created beauty, and though all created beauty is from God, and therefore must be in Him, yet it is in Him after a manner so different and perfect that there is no possibility of forming any just idea of the beauty of God in itself from what we see in creatures. Still there are several reasons which show us, in the most convincing manner, how great, how amazing, how infinitely delightful must be the beauty of God.

The Scriptures declare that God is the first author of beauty, and from thence draw the conclusion, if men be delighted with the beauty of the creatures, "Let them know how much the Lord of them is more beautiful than they; for the first author of beauty made all those things" (Wis. 13:3). "By the greatness of the beauty, and of the creature, the Creator of them may be seen, so as to be known thereby" (v. 5). This is a most just argument; for the Creator must have in Himself what he communicates to His creatures, and in a degree as much more perfect as He is infinitely more perfect and excellent than they.

If, therefore, the numberless beauties dispersed among creatures in the universe—the splendor of the sun, the brightness of the moon, the sparkling of the stars, the colors of the rainbow, the immense variety of beauty which we see in flowers, in the productions of the earth, in birds, beasts, and all living creatures—were all collected in one, and to this were added all the beauty that ever existed in the human form, yet all this would bear no more proportion to the uncreated beauty of God than a small fire to the sun, or a drop of water to the ocean.

Nay, what is still more, Almighty God not only is the author of all the beauty found in creatures which actually exist, but He can, if He please, create numbers of other worlds and of other creatures, as much exceeding the beauty of this universe as it exceeds a grain of sand. Consequently, He must contain in Himself all possible beauty without bounds or limitation, in presence of which the beauty of this world, and of thousands of worlds more perfect, would disappear as nothing as the stars in the presence of the sun. Hence Scripture says, "The moon shall blush and the sun shall be ashamed, when the Lord of hosts shall reign" (Is. 24:23). What an amazing idea does this give of the immensity of that Divine beauty and enjoyment of it must communicate to the souls of the blessed!

The second argument is taken from the properties of the Divine beauty. That it is altogether unchangeable, so that it is absolutely impossible it should ever fail, or even be in the smallest degree diminished. Oh, how frail and fading is all created beauty! Take that of the human form, the greatest and most engaging we know among creatures! How soon does a fit of sickness change the comeliest countenance into an object of horror! How does the short space of a few years deprive it of all its charms! Its color fades, its luster disappears, its liveliness decays, and as old age approaches and disfigures it, it can scarcely be recognized for what it was! Death at last puts an end to its existence and makes the most beautiful countenance even loathsome to behold!

What, then, is the beauty of man? A falling star, a fleeting meteor, a scene of inconstancy, the sport of time, the delusion of the eyes, a shining frailty! Not so the uncreated beauty of the great Creator; His Divine beauty is essential, unchangeable, eternal. No accident can lessen, no length of time diminish it, and the happy soul, once in possession of it, shall never be deprived of the inexpressible bliss she enjoys in contemplating it! The beauty of God is entire, perfect, pure, without the smallest mixture of deformity or imperfection.

Consider the most beautiful being that ever appeared in the world; how far is its beauty from being complete even in its own kind? With how many defects is it accompanied? And what innumerable other beauties are wanting to it? And after all it is only superficial, external, and under that outward appearance what does it contain? But the beauty of God is the assemblage of all possible beauty, in an infinite degree, without defect.

It is as impossible to add anything to its perfection as it is to diminish it!

It is superabundant so amazingly so that though it be communicated in different degrees to innumerable creatures, yet this causes no diminution of its own infinite perfection! Nay, it is so powerfully communicative that it transforms into its own likeness those happy souls who are admitted to its presence; for, "We all beholding the glory of the Lord with open face," says St. Paul, "are transformed into the same image" (2 Cor. 3:18). And if, therefore, the imperfect, fading, corruptible beauty of the creature has such an effect upon our hearts, and gives us such pleasure in beholding it, conceive, if you can, the amazing effect, the infinite delight, of seeing and possessing this uncreated, immense, essential, eternal beauty of the Creator!

The third argument to show the greatness of the beauty of God is taken from its effects on those who behold it; and these are two: incomprehensible pleasure and unbounded love. Pleasure and love are indeed the constant natural effects of beauty. It always gives a pleasure and delight to the heart of man. It naturally draws our will and affection towards it, and the more beautiful the object, the more powerfully does it produce these effects in our souls. Nothing, therefore, serves more to show us how immense must be the Divine beauty than to consider how it delights the souls of those who behold it, and how powerfully it draws to itself their love and affections.

Here we must observe that the pleasure and delight which the soul enjoys from the beatific vision of God is beyond explanation, indeed beyond conception: for, "From the beginning of the world they have not heard, nor perceived with the ears; the eye hath not seen, O God, besides Thee, what things Thou hast pre pared for them that wait for Thee" (Is. 64:4) or, as St. Paul expresses it, "The eye hath not seen, nor ear heard, neither hath it entered into the heart of man, what things God hath prepared for them that love Him" (1 Cor. 2:9). St. Paul also assures us that "the peace of God surpasses all understanding" (Phil. 4:7). So that the supreme delight which flows from contemplating the infinite beauty of God not only exceeds all the pleasures of this world but surpasses all that we can possibly conceive or imagine.

3

THE EXCELLENCE OF OUR LAST END

For who could ever imagine that He would so wonderfully exert His Almighty power, and employ the sovereign dominion He has over the whole creation to procure it, if [our salvation] were not an object of the highest excellence in His eyes, and worthy of all that He does to obtain it?

What we have already seen serves to give us the most sublime idea of the excellence of this glorious end for which we are created. For what can we conceive more exalted, more honorable, more glorious, than to be united with God by holy love. To be ever in His presence, enraptured with infinite delight in possessing Him, honored as His intimate friends and dear children, transformed into the image of His glory, and unchangeably fixed in the possession of that supreme good forever? However, as there are several other considerations which serve to show still more and more the invaluable excellence of our salvation, we shall here briefly state them.

The exalted light in which the Scriptures everywhere represents it to us. Thus our Savior says, "The kingdom of heaven is like unto a treasure hidden in a field, which when a man hath found he hides, and for joy thereof goes and sells all that he hath, and buys that field. Again, the kingdom of heaven is like to a merchant seeking good pearls; who when he had found one pearl of great price, went his way, and sold all that he had, and bought it" (Matt. 12:44). In both these similitudes Jesus Christ Himself shows us of what infinite value our salvation is; nothing in this world can be comparable to it.

Consider the words of our Lord: "Blessed are those servants, whom the Lord, when He cometh, shall find watching; Amen, I say to you, that He will gird Himself, and make them sit down to meat, and passing will minister to them" (Luke 12:37). What an inconceivable idea does this expression of the Son of God give of the dignity and honor which He will bestow on His faithful servants! He Himself will become, in a manner, their servant.

This is further shown from the extraordinary means which God has used, and daily uses, for procuring the salvation of His elect. For who could ever imagine that He would so wonderfully exert His Almighty power, and employ the sovereign dominion He has over the whole creation to procure it, if it were not an object of the highest excellence in His eyes and worthy of all that He does to obtain it?

On this, then, we must observe that the creation of this world, and all the wondrous ways of Divine Providence preserving and governing it, are intended for the salvation of souls, as the great end the Creator has in view in its existence. The inferior creatures are intended for the use and benefit of man, to display to him the wisdom, power, goodness, and other perfections of the Creator. Thus, creation serves as motives, means, or instruments by which man may be excited and enabled to know, love, and glorify his God, and by so doing save his own soul.

What wonderful things did God do in all parts of the creation in the heavens, in the earth, in the seas and rivers in order to bring His chosen people out of Egypt, and place them in the earthly Canaan, the land of promise. All these things were done in figure of us, to show the economy of the Divine Providence in what

He does to bring His elect from the Egypt of sin, and from the bondage of Satan, and place them in the heavenly Canaan, the true land of promise.

How exalted an idea does all this give us of the great value and excellence of the salvation of souls when we see the Almighty using such wonderful means to procure it and making all creation subservient to it! Nothing is of any value in the sight of God but salvation; everything else in comparison of it is with Him an object of contempt.

But what are those means used by God to procure the salvation of souls in comparison with what Jesus Christ, the Son of God, has done and suffered for that purpose? He has not the smallest need of us, and that when we have done all, we must acknowledge ourselves unprofitable servants; when we consider this, and then behold this great Being, when we were lost in sin, humbling Himself, taking upon Him the form of man, in the likeness of sinful flesh (see Rom. 8) and after suffering the most cruel and ignominious torments, at last dying in a disgraceful manner upon a cross to save our souls, and bring them to eternal salvation, we are confounded, we are lost in amazement! Think what we please, we shall never be able to fathom this incomprehensible mystery but will be forced to conclude that the salvation of souls must be a valuable object indeed, since the eternal wisdom of the Father used such extraordinary means to procure it.

Another thing which shows the immense value and excellence of salvation is that it is eternal; in which respect the greatest and most esteemed things of this world disappear in its presence as smoke before the wind. And, indeed, what weight or value can any human affair have in the heart of a thinking man when he reflects that it must all soon end? How vain do all the toils and labors of men appear, even in those affairs which seem to them of the highest importance, when we reflect how soon their greatest achievements and most renowned performances are brought to nothing!

What labors, what toils, what dangers, what waste of blood and treasure did it not cost an Alexander, a Caesar, and other worldly heroes to conquer kingdoms and establish empires? And yet how short was the time that they enjoyed the fruit of their labors! How soon after their death were the conquests lost and their very countries themselves sunk in obscurity! Nothing appears more reasonable, or of greater consequence in the eyes of worldly people, than to spend their time and labor in improving their fortunes, raising their families, and laying up treasure for their children. But how often are they disappointed in their views, notwithstanding all their endeavors? And if they do succeed, how long does it last? Scarce a generation passes when their posterity, either by their own folly or unforeseen accidents, are reduced to poverty, misery, and obscurity.

4

THE IMPORTANCE OF OUR LAST END

Our salvation is not only our own business, the affair that properly belongs to ourselves, but it is, in fact, our only necessary business, the only thing for which we were sent into this world.

It is a matter of the greatest importance to us to secure our salvation. Indeed, it is the only affair of importance we have to think of, as will evidently appear from several convincing arguments. From its own excellence, which we have already seen, and on which we may here observe, that there is nothing wherein the goodness of God towards us appears in more amiable colors than in the glorious end for which He has created us. Other creatures around us on the earth have their being only for this world and must end with time, but man is made to live when time shall be no more, and all shall be swallowed up in eternity.

We are placed in this world for no other end than to work out our salvation. Our time here will be but for a few years at most. We are here in this life only as in a place of banishment, kept at a distance from our heavenly country, our eternal habitation. We ought therefore to look upon ourselves here only as pilgrims and strangers left in this world as in a place of probation, where our great business is to fit and prepare ourselves for eternal bliss, to labor in this vineyard that we may obtain the promised reward, to run in the race which is set before us that we may gain the prize, to fight against the enemies of our soul that we may secure to ourselves the incorruptible crown. This is our business here, our great work.

Our salvation is not only our own business, the affair that properly belongs to ourselves, but it is, in fact, our only necessary business, the only thing for which we were sent into this world. Our blessed Savior declares this in His answer to Martha when she seemed displeased at seeing her sister Mary so taken up with hearing Him that she left her to toil alone: "Martha, Martha," said He, "thou art careful, and art troubled about many things; but one thing is necessary: Mary hath chosen the best part" (Luke 10:41).

Our salvation is the one thing necessary; everything is trifling in comparison to this, and of no importance whether it be done or not, if we can only secure salvation. This is the necessary business of all mankind, of the king and the beggar, the rich and the poor, the learned and the ignorant. It is nowise necessary that a man be rich, learned, or great in the world, that he be of this or that employment, in one state of life or another, but it is absolutely necessary for all to work out their salvation.

The vast importance and necessity of our salvation is principally shown from the dreadful consequences of losing it. "What will it profit a man," says Jesus Christ Himself, "if he gain the whole world, and lose his own soul? Or what shall a man give in exchange for his soul?" (Mark 8:36).

Suppose yourself master of the whole universe, how soon must your enjoyment of this end! When you die, what will it profit if you be buried in hell-fire and condemned for ever to those eternal flames, where the worm dies not and the fire is not extinguished. Where there shall be nothing but weeping, and wailing, and gnashing of teeth. Where fire, and brimstone, and snares shall be the portion of their cup. Where they shall be filled with drunkenness and sorrow, with the cup of grief and sadness, and be made to drink it up even to the dregs. Where they shall be salted with fire. Where they shall have no rest night or day, no comfort, no peace, no ease no, not so much as a single drop of water to cool their parched tongues. Where they shall seek death and shall not find it they shall desire to die, and death shall fly from them. Where they shall gnaw their tongues for pain. Gracious God!

What a complication of miseries is this! Yet this is what the Word of God assures us will be the eternal portion of those who lose their salvation. What madness and folly, then, must it be to neglect that great, that important affair, or to expose it to the smallest danger of being lost, for any consideration in this world!

5

THE DIFFICULTY OF ACQUIRING OUR LAST END

Worldly-minded persons who live in sin, and lukewarm Christians who live in a kind of indifference about their souls, have great need indeed to be roused from their insensibility and encouraged by every consideration which can make any impression upon them.

The truth is, the road to salvation is both difficult and easy. To acquire salvation is a most difficult matter to those who are slaves to their passions, attached to the enjoyments of this world, and immersed in sensuality and carnal pleasures. But it is easy to those who know its value and place their affections on God and eternal goods. It is difficult to flesh and blood, and to all the perverse dispositions of our corrupt nature, but it is easy to a man who, by Christian vigilance and repeated victories over nature, has corrected the disorders of the heart and brought the body into proper subjection.

Those who have surrendered to Christ are carried on by the wings of holy love, and knowing from their own blessed experience what happiness is found in the service of God, they are ready to sacrifice all that is near or dear to them in this world rather than abandon it. Nay, the more they have to suffer for God's sake, the more their joy and consolation abound. But worldly-minded persons who live in sin, and lukewarm Christians who live in a kind of indifference about their souls, have great need indeed to be roused from their insensibility, and encouraged by every consideration which can make any impression upon them.

At the same time, it would be a dangerous encouragement and fatal delusion to lead them to imagine that securing their salvation is a matter of no difficulty and that they can attend to it at any time they please. To them the great work of salvation is a work of difficulty and requires the strongest resolution and their utmost efforts to do anything effectual in it. And the longer they delay, the greater the difficulty becomes; for by delay their bad habits are strengthened, their passions become more violent. But however great the difficulty may be at present, it ought the more effectually to incite them to begin that great work without delay. Their all is at stake; the delay of a day may prove their eternal ruin! Certainly it will make their labor more difficult!

We have seen the immense value of salvation, how unspeakably important it is, and that obedience to the commands of God is absolutely necessary to obtain it. What a powerful motive to make us diligent and solicitous to obey them! Our eternal happiness depends upon our obedience; there is no salvation without it. How strongly, then, does both duty and interest combine to incite us to it! We are obliged to obey Him for our own interest, because our real happiness in this world, and our eternal happiness in the world to come, depend entirely upon our doing so. But is it possible we can believe these truths, and yet offend our God, or ever dare to transgress His commandments? One would think it impossible that a Christian who believes these truths could ever offend God. But how comes it that Christians are so unhappy as to do so?

PART 2

THE ENEMIES OF OUR SALVATION

6

THE FIRST ENEMY: THE FLESH

Our own flesh is certainly the most dangerous of the three, both because it is a domestic enemy which we always carry about us, and cannot fly from, and also because it is principally by its means that the other two gain so easily the advantage over us.

The unhappiness of Christians believing in these truths is owing to the power and malice of the enemies of our salvation and to the negligence of Christians in not fortifying themselves against their snares by serious meditation on the truths of eternity and other holy exercises. By this neglect their faith in the above truths becomes languid and dead. Thus, they fall an easy prey to these enemies and are dragged by them, like sheep to the slaughter, into eternal ruin. These enemies are the devil, the world, and the flesh, on each of which we shall make some few useful observations.

Our own flesh is certainly the most dangerous of the three, both because it is a domestic enemy which we always carry about us, and cannot fly from, and also because it is principally by its means that the other two gain so easily the advantage over us. Now on this we must observe, by the flesh is meant our corrupt nature, our selflove, and all its passions, that bent and propensity of our nature to everything which gratifies our sensuality and pride. In a word, it is our love and attachment to the enjoyments of this life, to understand which we must remember that it is the great and essential duty of all mankind, arising from their very existence itself, and from the end for which they were created, to love, serve, and obey God, to study in everything to please Him, and "whether they eat or drink, or whatever else they do, to do all to His glory," and to fulfil the will of Him that made them.

In the state of innocence man had no difficulty in fulfilling this duty. His heart was upright with God, he had Him before his eyes in all he did, and it was his delight to please Him continually. But by sin we lost that happy union with God; our hearts were corrupted and violently bent upon seeking their own pleasure, interest, and glory instead of the interest, pleasure, and glory of God. Hence arises that strong attachment to riches, to sensual pleasure, to the liberty of acting according to our own will, to the esteem and praise of the world, to curiosity, to ease, and to everything else that is pleasing and agreeable to nature, and this is what is meant by the flesh or self-love.

Now, as the whole tendency of the law of God is to recover our lost union with God, and to bring back our love and affection to Him, and as this is diametrically opposed to the inclinations of self-love, we find great difficulty in complying with the law of God and experience violent opposition from ourselves in doing so. Our love of liberty can brook no restraint. Our pride, our avarice, our love of ease and pleasure strongly incline us to seek only such objects as are pleasing, and these passions, being deeply interwoven with our nature, blind our reason, or engage it to favor them, and hurry us on to act for their own satisfaction, forgetful or regardless of God and of what we owe to Him. The Scriptures reduce all our depraved affections to three general heads: the lust of the eye, the lust of the flesh, and the pride of life. These are the three great branches of self-love.

The effects which self-love and its lusts produce in the soul are many and dangerous. They darken our understanding and pervert our judgment, persuading us that those things are real goods which flatter self-love and gratify its lusts, and that those things are real evils which are contrary and disagreeable to it. They call light darkness, and darkness light; they call sweet bitter, and bitter sweet, as Scripture expresses it. They pervert our reason, and engage it to favor their pretensions, by numberless plausible arguments which have nothing solid in them. They fill the imagination with innumerable ideas of vain, idle, dangerous, and sinful objects, and fix them there with inveterate obstinacy, rendering it difficult and painful to fix our thoughts and attention upon spiritual things.

Our free will, which naturally follows the light presented to it by the understanding, being thus surrounded by a darkened understanding, a depraved reason, and a sensual imagination, is in a manner irresistibly attracted to those objects which gratify self-love. All the passions of the soul are engaged to favor self-love and defend its usurped authority: hope, fear, joy, sorrow, anger, hatred, despair, and the whole train of their attendants, employed by turns in its service, hurry on the soul to commit numberless sins against the law of God, in disregard of all we owe to Him.

The more the soul acts from these impulses of self-love, the more the above evils are increased; the understanding becomes more blind, the reason more perverted, and the will more enslaved. A habit of evil is contracted in all the powers of the soul, and the opposition thus raised to salvation is inconceivable. The sinner even sports with iniquity, loves his delusion, and despises whatever could tend to undeceive him.

The Holy Scriptures describe this unhappy corruption of our nature by sin: "This I have found," says Solomon, "that God made man right, and he hath entangled himself with an infinity of questions" (Eccles. 7:30). "All that is in the world is the concupiscence of the flesh, and the concupiscence of the eyes, and the pride of life" (1 John 2:16). "The wickedness of man is great upon the earth, and all the thought of their heart is bent upon evil at all times" (Gen. 6:5). "For the imagination and thought of man's heart are prone to evil from his youth" (Gen. 8:21).

"They were deceived; for their own malice blinded them, and they knew not the secrets of God, nor hoped for the wages of justice, nor esteemed the honor of holy souls" (Wis. 2:21). "For the bewitching of vanity obscures good things, and the wandering of concupiscence overturns the innocent mind" (Wis. 4:12). "When they knew God, they have not glorified Him as God, or given thanks; but became vain in their thoughts, and their foolish heart was darkened" (Rom. 1:21). "They walk in the vanity of their mind, having their understanding darkened, being alienated from the life of God, through the ignorance that is in them, because of the blindness of their hearts. Who, despairing, have given themselves up to lasciviousness, to the working of all uncleanness, unto covetousness" (Eph. 4:17); but "Woe to you that call evil good, and good evil; that put darkness for light, and light for darkness; that put bitter for sweet, and sweet for bitter" (Is. 5:20).

"Men love darkness rather than light, for their works are evil: for every one that doth evil hateth the light, and cometh not to the light, that his works may not be reproved" (John 3:19). "A fool worketh mischief as it were for sport" (Prov. 10:23). "They leave the right way, and walk by dark ways; who are glad when they have done evil, and rejoice when they have done most wicked things" (Prov. 2:13). "If the Ethiopian can change his skin, or the leopard his spots, you also may do well when you have learned evil" (Jer. 13:23). "The wicked man, when he is come into the depth of sins, contempt; but ignominy and reproach follow him" (Prov. 18:3); for "the man that with a stiff neck despises him that reproves him, shall suddenly be destroyed, and health shall not follow him" (Prov. 29:1).

To avoid these evils, and overcome the snares that our self-love and its concupiscence lay for our souls, two things are absolutely necessary, and are the arms by which alone we can defend ourselves against its attacks. One is frequent meditation upon the doctrine of Jesus Christ on this subject, and to excite in our souls a lively conviction of the vanity of earthly enjoyments and the misery they bring here and hereafter if we seek our happiness in them. But this alone will not suffice. For though we be persuaded of these truths, yet so long as our hearts are enslaved to the bewitching pleasures of the senses, they will drag us into sin in spite of all we know, and our attachment will never be broken so long as we continue to gratify self-love by indulging its desires.

The second thing required is continual self-denial, to deprive our self-love of those things which are agreeable to sensuality and pride, and to force it to undergo things which are unpleasant and humbling, according to the repeated injunctions laid upon us by the Word of God. And hence we see the goodness of our blessed

Savior in obliging all His followers to deny themselves to take up their cross and crucify their flesh as a necessary condition of being His disciples. However disagreeable these things are to nature, yet they are necessary for obtaining eternal happiness. This Jesus Christ knows, and therefore out of love for our souls, and zeal for our eternal happiness, He lays these commands upon us, knowing that, if left to our own choice, we would never have resolution to practice these rigorous virtues.

7

THE SECOND ENEMY: THE WORLD

They call light darkness, and darkness light; they call sweet bitter, and bitter sweet. . . . They pervert our reason, and engage it to favor their pretensions, by numberless plausible arguments which have nothing solid in them. They fill the imagination with innumerable ideas of vain, idle, dangerous, and sinful objects, and fix them there with inveterate obstinacy, rendering it difficult and painful to fix our thoughts and attention upon spiritual things.

The second enemy of our salvation is the world, on which we must observe that by the world is understood the great bulk of mankind who live in the captivity and bondage of self-love, blinded by its delusions. Slaves to its passions and concupiscence; not only following individually its suggestions, but joining as a body in making an open profession of doing so. They propagate the false maxims of self-love and praise sensual enjoyments as the only real good. They praise riches, honors, and the pleasures of life as the only things worthy of our notice, esteeming and honoring those who have the greatest abundance of them, despising and undervaluing those who have them not. They turn everything into ridicule which is contrary to their own false opinions. "They are of the world: therefore of the world they speak, and the world hears them" (1 John 4:5).

The world, then, is a tumultuous multitude of persons of various characters and tastes, who, rejecting the maxims of the Gospel of Jesus Christ, have no object in view but their own interest, no rule for their conduct but their passions, nothing that interests them but the riches, the pleasures, or the honors of this life. They openly profess themselves enemies of piety and devotion. They think themselves at liberty to deride virtue, to ridicule the most venerable practices of piety, to glory in their dissolute conduct, and to boast of irreligion. Among this confused multitude there reigns universal dissimulation, by which they deceive and impose on one another.

The Word of God gives us a most dreadful description of this great enemy of souls: "God looked down from heaven on the children of men, to see if there were any that did understand, or did seek God. All of them have gone aside; they are become unprofitable together; there is none that doth good, no, not one" (Ps. 52:3). "I have seen iniquity and contradiction in the city. Day and night shall iniquity surround it upon its walls, and in the midst thereof are labor and injustice; and usury and deceit have not departed from its streets. . . . Their words are smoother than oil, and the same are darts" (Ps. 54:10, 22). "The sons of men, whose teeth are weapons and arrows, and their tongue a sharp sword" (Ps. 56:5). "Vain are the sons of men; the sons of men are liars in the balances, that by vanity they may together deceive" (Ps. 61:10). "All that is in the world is the concupiscence of the flesh, the concupiscence of the eyes, and the pride of life; which is not of the Father, but is of the world" (1 John 2:16). "We know that we are of God, and the whole world is seated in wickedness" (1 John 5:19).

Jesus Christ, "the True Light which enlightens every man that cometh into this world; He was in the world, and the world was made by Him, and the world knew Him not" (John 1:9). "Neither does it know God the

Father" (John 17:25). "The world cannot receive the Holy Ghost, the Spirit of Truth, because it sees Him not, nor knows Him" (John 14:17). It hates Jesus Christ and His faithful followers. "If the world hate you," says He, "know that it hath hated Me before you. If you had been of the world, the world would love its own; but because you are not of the world, but I have chosen you out of the world, therefore the world hates you" (John 15:18).

"There is a generation," says Solomon, "that are pure in their own eyes, and yet are not washed from their filthiness; a generation whose eyes are lofty, and their eyelids lifted up on high. A generation, that for teeth hath swords, and grinds with their jaw-teeth, to devour the needy from off the earth, and the poor from among men" (Prov. 30:12). And David, thanking God for having been protected from them, speaks thus: "Thou hast protected me from the assembly of the malignant; from the multitude of the workers of iniquity. For they have whetted their tongues like a sword; they have bent their bow, a bitter thing, to shoot in secret the undefiled. They shall shoot at him on a sudden, and will not fear; they are resolute in wickedness. They have talked of hiding snares; they have said, who shall see them?" (Ps. 63:3). "They are enemies," says St. Paul, "of the cross of Christ; whose end is destruction; whose god is their belly; whose glory is in their shame; who mind earthly things" (Phil. 3:18). Says St. James, "Know you not that the friendship of this world is the enmity of God? Whosoever, therefore, will be a friend of this world, becometh an enemy of God" (Jas. 4:4).

Though this unhappy world, this declared enemy of Jesus Christ and of His cross, usurps an unlimited authority and exercises a cruel tyranny over the hearts of men, yet, it is amazing to see how it is loved and followed, its favor courted, and its frowns dreaded, even by those who pretend to despise it and are ashamed in their hearts of their base subjection to it. The world promises to its votaries all earthly happiness, riches, pleasures, and honors in abundance praise, esteem, and favor of men, and everything else that can flatter and gratify self-love. As our natural attachment to these things is strong and violent, we eagerly adopt its maxims, grasp at its offers, and come into its measures in order to obtain them.

On the other hand, it threatens the greatest misery to those who withstand it, pointing them out as objects of contempt, and as there is nothing so wounding to our pride as contempt and ridicule, so there is nothing which more effectually undermines our virtue and shakes our best resolutions than this powerful engine when employed against us. Hence the power which these common expressions have over even the best of people, "What will the world say? What will men think of us?" Hence the opposition which we meet with to a life of virtue and piety from our own heart, our ready compliance with the ways of the world, and the many excuses which our reason, engaged on the side of self-love, invents and urges to justify this compliance.

The Scriptures describe these deluding arts of the world and tell us how great is its hatred against the servants of God: "The wicked loathe them that are in the right way" (Prov. 29:27). "He that walketh in the right way and fears God, is despised by him that goes by an infamous way" (Prov. 14:2). "The simplicity of the just man is laughed to scorn" (Job 12:4). Then it shows us what arts it uses to corrupt the good and the cause of its hatred against them: "They have said, reasoning with themselves, but not right: The time of our life is short and tedious, and in the end of a man there is no remedy; and no man hath been known to return from hell. For we are all born of nothing, and after this we shall be as if we had never been: for the breath of our nostrils is smoke, and speech a spark to move our heart, which being put out, our body shall be ashes, and our spirit shall be poured abroad as soft air; and our life shall pass away as the trace of a cloud, and shall be dispersed as a mist, which is driven away by the beams of the sun, and overpowered with the heat thereof; and our name in time shall be forgotten, and no man shall have any remembrance of our works. For our time is as the passing of a shadow, and there is no going back of our end; for it is fast sealed, and no man returns. Come, therefore, and let us enjoy the good things that are present, and let us speedily use the creatures as in youth. Let us fill ourselves with costly wine and ointments, and let not the flower of the time pass by us. Let us crown ourselves with roses before they be withered; let no meadow escape our riot. Let none of us go without his part in luxury: let us everywhere leave tokens of joy; for this is our portion, and this our lot" (Wis. 2:1–9).

Does not this passage seem intended to describe not only the substance of what the world says but even the very words it uses to deceive souls?

Oh, how many are deluded to their eternal ruin by such allurements! For "evil communications corrupt good manners" (1 Cor. 15:33). But if the just withstand this assault, see how the world shifts its ground, and attacks them with other weapons! "Let us oppress the poor just man, and not spare the widow, nor honor the ancient grey hairs of the aged. Let our strength be the law of justice, for that which is feeble is found to be nothing worth. Let us therefore lie in wait for the just, because he is not for our turn, and he is contrary to our doings, and upbraids us with transgressions of the law, and divulges against us the sins of our way of life. He boasts that he hath the knowledge of God, and calls himself the son of God. He is become a censurer of our thoughts. He is grievous unto us even to behold; for his life is not like other men's, and his ways are very different. We are esteemed by him as triflers, and he abstains from our ways as from filthiness. Let us see, then, if his words be true, and let us prove what shall happen to him, and we shall know what his end shall be. . . . Let us examine him by outrages and tortures, that we may know his meekness and try his patience. . . . These things they thought, and were deceived, for their malice blinded them" (Wis. 2:10–21).

David also describes this conduct of the worldly man, and the fatal success he too often has against good people, in these words: "His mouth is full of cursing, and of bitterness, and of deceit: under his tongue are labor and sorrow. He sits in ambush with the rich in private places, that he may kill the innocent. His eyes are upon the poor man: he lieth in wait in secret, like a lion in his den. He lieth in ambush that he may catch the poor man, to catch the poor whilst he draws him to him. In his net he will bring him down, he will crouch and fall, when he shall have power over the poor" (Ps. 9:28–31).

It is manifest that the power of these engines which the world uses to draw us from our duty and the service of God is owing to our self-love and our slavish attachment to worldly enjoyments. For if we had no attachment to the riches and pleasures of life, if we were truly humble of heart like our Lord and Master, if we were lovers of the cross of Christ, as His servants ought to be, the world, with all its engines, could make no impression on us. We would despise its deluding promises and scorn its empty threats.

Hence the most effectual remedy against all its snares is to nourish in our hearts a lively faith in the truths of eternity; for "this is the victory which overcomes the world, our faith" (1 Jn. 5:4). By the constant exercise of self-denial and mortification, to "take off our affections from things below, and set them on the things above, where Christ sits on the right hand of God" (Col. 3:1). And in this we see again with how much reason our blessed Savior so strictly requires the practice of self-denial from all His followers.

Besides, the Scriptures give us several important injunctions on this subject. To fly from the world, as far as circumstances permit, and to take no part in its alluring amusements: thus "My son, if sinners shall entice thee, consent not to them. If they say, Come with us, let us lie in wait for blood, let us hide snares for the innocent without cause; let us swallow him up alive like hell, and whole as one that goes down into the pit; we shall find all precious substance, we shall fill our houses with spoils. Cast in thy lot with us; let us all have one purse. My son, walk not thou with them; restrain thy foot from their paths: for their feet run to evil" (Prov. 1:10). "Be not delighted in the paths of the wicked, neither let the way of evil men please thee; flee from it, pass not by it, go aside and forsake it" (Prov. 4:24).

Never to court the favor of the world, nor do the least thing contrary to our duty in order to please it. "Do I speak to please men?" says the apostle St. Paul; "if I yet pleased men, I should not be the servant of Christ" (Gal. 1:10). "They have not called upon God; there have they trembled for fear, where there was no fear: for God hath scattered the bones of them that please men: they have been confounded, because God hath despised them" (Ps. 52:6). "Love not the world, nor the things that are in the world: if any man loves the world, the charity of the Father is not in him" (1 Jn. 2:15). "Whosoever will be a friend of this world becomes an enemy of God" (Jas. 4:4).

Never to fear the world, nor any of its evils, but to oppose to the base fear of the world the wholesome fear of God. "I say to you, my friends" (these are the words of Jesus Christ to His faithful followers), "Be not afraid of them that kill the body, and after that have no more that they can do. But I will show you Whom you shall fear: fear ye Him Who, after He hath killed, hath power to cast into hell. Yea, I say to you, Fear Him" (Luke 12:4). And God Himself by His prophet: "Hearken to me," says He, "you that know what is just; My people, who have My law in your heart: fear ye not the reproach of men, and be not afraid of their blasphemies; for the worm shall eat them up as a garment, and the moth shall consume them as wool; but My salvation shall be forever, and My justice from generation to generation" (Is. 51:7).

"And thou, O son of man, fear not, neither be thou afraid of their words; for thou art among unbelievers and destroyers, and thou dwellest with scorpions. Fear not their words, neither be thou dismayed at their looks; for they are a provoking house" (Ezech. 2:6). To despise the opinion of the world, and whatever it may think or say of us, and to study only to please God. "I am not troubled," says Jeremiah to God, "following Thee, my pastor, and I have not desired the day of man; Thou knows it: that which went out of my lips hath been right in Thy sight" (Jer. 17:16).

"With me," says St. Paul, "it is a very small thing to be judged by you, or by man's day . . . but He that judges me is the Lord" (1 Cor. 4:3). "Woe to you, when men shall bless you; for according to these things did their fathers to the false prophets" (Luke 6:26). "And the Lord said, where unto shall I liken the men of this generation, and to what are they like? They are like to children sitting in the marketplace, and speaking one to another, and saying, We have piped to you, and you have not danced; we have mourned, and you have not wept. For John the Baptist came neither eating bread nor drinking wine; and you say he hath a devil. The Son of Man is come eating and drinking; and you say, Behold a man that is a glutton and a drinker of wine, a friend of tax collectors and sinners; and wisdom is justified by all her children" (Luke 7:31–35). So malicious is the world that it will censure and blame whatever one does, and therefore its judgments deserve no regard, being founded in caprice and not in justice. It is also variable, inconstant, and never to be depended upon.

The same world that received Jesus Christ into Jerusalem as a great prophet with hosannas and acclamations, a few days after cried out, "Crucify Him! Crucify Him!" as an infamous malefactor. How unworthy, then, of our regard are the judgments of the world! By no means to imitate the world, nor conform ourselves to its customs and ways. To glory in standing up for the cause of God, and even to rejoice in having anything to suffer from the world on that account.

"And if also you suffer anything for justice's sake, blessed are ye. And be not afraid of their terror, and be not troubled; but sanctify the Lord Christ in your hearts, being ready always to satisfy everyone that asks you a reason of that hope that is in you" (1 Ptr. 3:14). "Arise," says God to His prophet, "arise, and speak to them all that I command thee. Be not afraid of their presence, for I will make thee not to be afraid of their countenance" (Jer. 1:17).

8

THE THIRD ENEMY: THE DEVIL

As he was a liar from the beginning, he chiefly makes use of lies and falsehoods to deceive and ensnare us, sometimes by himself, and sometimes by means of wicked men, whom he uses as his apostles.

The third enemy of our salvation is the devil, concerning whom the following particulars are to be known. The account which the Scriptures give of him, his character and dispositions. "Our wrestling," says St. Paul, "is not against flesh and blood, but against principalities and powers; against the rulers of the world of this darkness, against the spirits of wickedness in the high places" (Eph. 6:12). And in other places of Scripture, the devil, who is the chief of these spirits of darkness, is called the prince of this world, and of him it is said, "There is no power upon earth that can be compared with him, who was made to fear no one. He beholds every high thing, and is king over all the children of pride" (Job 41:24). "By the envy of the evil, death came into the world" (Wis. 2:24); for "he was a murderer from the beginning, and he abode not in the truth, because the truth is not in him. When he speaks a lie, he speaks of his own; for he is a liar, and the father of lies" (John 8:44).

He has an implacable hatred to man and is continually seeking to ruin him: "Behold Satan hath desired to have you, that he may sift you as wheat" (Luke 22:31); for "your adversary the devil, as a roaring lion, goes about seeking whom he may devour" (1 Ptr. 5:8) and is the cause of innumerable woes to man: "Woe to the earth and to the sea, because the devil is come down to you, having a great wrath, knowing that he hath but a short time" (Apoc. 12:12). When he gets souls into his power he keeps them captive, and drags them on at his will to all sin" (2 Tim. 2:26). "You were dead in your offences and sins, wherein, in time past, you walked according to the course of this world, according to the prince of the power of this air, of the spirit that now worketh on the children of unbelief" (Eph. 2:1).

Concerning the nature of his temptations, we are told that he blinds the understanding and makes us forget or not advert to the great truths of eternity: "The god of this world hath blinded the minds of unbelievers, that the light of the Gospel of the glory of Christ, Who is the image of God, should not shine unto them" (2 Cor. 4:4). To effect this, he gives them an aversion to hearing the Word of God, according to what our Savior says to the Jews, "You are of your father the devil, and the desire of your father you will do. . . . He that is of God, heareth the words of God; therefore you hear them not, because you are not of God" (John 8:44, 47). And when at any time they do hear them, "The devil cometh and taketh the word out of their heart, lest believing they should be saved" (Luke 8:12).

As he was a liar from the beginning, he chiefly makes use of lies and falsehoods to deceive and ensnare us, sometimes by himself, and sometimes by means of wicked men, whom he uses as his apostles. For this purpose, "False apostles," says St. Paul, "are deceitful workmen, transforming themselves into the apostles of Christ: and no wonder, for Satan frequently transforms himself into an angel of light" (2 Cor. 11:13). Sometimes he makes use of the Word of God itself, as he did to Jesus Christ Himself when he tempted Him in the wilderness. Sometimes he deceives by lying signs and wonders, as will be the case chiefly towards the end of the world, when his delusions will be "so great as to deceive, if possible, even the elect" (Matt. 24:24; 2 Thess. 2:9, 10).

But we are told that the main source of his temptations, and of the fatal weakness which gives him too often the advantage over us, is our self-love, our passions and attachments to the things of this world. Hence, his attacks are always pointed at this quarter by proposing some worldly good to engage our self-love on his side, or threatening some temporal evil to deter us. Thus, he attacked our first parents in Paradise by what was flattering to pride: "You shall be as gods," said he (Gen. 3:5). He induced David to number his people by vanity: "And Satan rose up against Israel, and moved David to number Israel" (1 Par. 21:1).

Through the love of money, "the devil put it into the heart of Judas to betray Christ" (John 12:2). Through the same means, "Satan tempted the heart of Ananias and Saphira to lie to the Holy Ghost, and by fraud to keep part of the price of their lands" (Acts 5:3). When he tempted Christ Himself, he attacked Him by the same allurements: first of pleasure, then of vainglory, and lastly of avarice. And indeed it is evident that were it not for our self-love he could have no weapon to attack us, nor would his temptations make any impression on us. For if we neither desired those things which are flattering to self-love nor feared what is contrary to it, it is plain that neither promises of the one nor threats of the other could ever move us from our duty. We therefore see that the principal defense against all his temptations is to conquer our self-love by continual mortification.

But as this is a remedy requiring great courage, Scripture points out several others which practically assist us in applying it. Sobriety or temperance, by which, if we have not resolution to mortify our self-love entirely, we restrain it at least within the bounds of moderation and never allow it to drag us to excess. Watching, by keeping a continual guard over our heart to observe the first motion of any temptation, and reject it entirely, never allowing our thoughts to dwell upon it, but doing with it as we would with a spark of fire falling upon our clothe—that is, to shake it off immediately.

"Blessed is the man that shall take thy little ones" (these beginnings of temptations) "and dash them against the rock" (Ps. 136: 9) by a speedy recourse to the rock, which is Christ—that is, by flying to Him with a strong faith and confidence in God, distrusting ourselves as unable to do any good without Him, and imploring His assistance by humble and fervent prayer—for "God resists the proud, but gives grace to the humble" (Jas. 4:6). A firm and unwearied resistance against the enemy, however long his attacks continue, never yielding in the smallest degree to his suggestions, even in the most trifling matters.

Of all these remedies, Scripture speaks as follows: "Take unto you the armor of God, that you may be able to resist in the evil day, and to stand in all things perfect. Stand therefore, having your loins girt about with truth, and having on the breastplate of justice, and your feet shod with the preparation of the gospel of peace. In all things taking the shield of faith, wherewith you may be able to extinguish all the fiery darts of the wicked one. And take unto you the helmet of salvation, and the sword of the Spirit which is the Word of God: by all prayer and supplication, praying at all times in the Spirit, and in the same watching with all instance" (Eph. 6:13).

"Be subject to God; but resist the devil, and he will fly from you. Draw nigh to God, and He will draw nigh to you" (Jas 4:7). "Be you humbled, therefore, under the mighty hand of God, that He may exalt you in the time of visitation; casting all your care upon Him, for

He hath care of you. Be sober and watch; because your adversary the devil, as a roaring lion, goes about seeking whom he may devour: whom resist ye, strong in faith" (1 Ptr. 5:6). "Watch ye and pray, that ye enter not into temptation" (Matt. 26:41). "He that fears God, neglects nothing" (Ecclus. 7:19); for "he that contemns small things, shall fall by little and little" (Ecclus. 19:1).

9

ANOTHER PRECAUTION: OCCASIONS OF SIN

Hence these dangerous occasions are called in Scriptural language the evil way, the road to sin, the way of iniquity; for as the road or way to any place leads those who walk in it to that place, so these dangerous occasions lead those who walk in them to wickedness and sin.

There is yet another precaution to be observed with the utmost care to fortify us against the assaults of our spiritual enemies, so necessary because the others will be of little service without it, and that is, carefully to fly from and avoid all the dangerous occasions of sin. On this important subject the following things are to be considered.

By the occasions of sin are meant those circumstances in which a man is exposed to the danger of committing sin. Thus, for example, a tavern is an occasion of sin to a drunkard, insomuch that it will be morally impossible for him to reclaim himself while he frequents it. Gaming, besides its own intrinsic evil, exposes to the danger of anger, cursing, and swearing; immodest discourses to impure thoughts and desires; the conversation of unbelievers to doubts concerning points of faith; reading bad books to take pleasure in, or consent to, the evil they contain; the company and conversation of those who curse and swear to speak in the same disgusting manner.

Hence these dangerous occasions are called in Scriptural language the evil way, the road to sin, the way of iniquity; for as the road or way to any place leads those who walk in it to that place, so these dangerous occasions lead those who walk in them to wickedness and sin. Thus David says, "Remove from me the way of iniquity" (Ps. 118:29); "I have restrained my feet from every evil way, that I may keep Thy words" (v. 101); "I have hated every way of iniquity" (v. 104); and the wise man, "Go not," says he, "in the way of ruin, and thou shall not stumble against the stones" (Ecclus. 32:25).

How difficult, or rather morally impossible, it is to expose one's self to these dangerous occasions and not be led away by them, is manifest from experience itself; for when a thing is actually present with us, it has much greater power to excite our passions than when absent; and we find it infinitely more difficult to restrain these passions in the presence of the object that excites them than when it is distant from us. A person who is moderately hungry feels the cravings of his appetite, but he can easily bear them, but set some savory meat before him, and he will scarcely be able to refrain from it. Just so when one is in the dangerous occasion of sin by its presence, it acts so strongly upon the senses, and so excites the sensual appetite, as easily to drag away the will to consent to those sins which it proposes.

Suppose a person loses his money in gaming; he is vexed at his misfortune, he condemns his folly, and resolves to renounce that delusive amusement. If he avoid the occasion, he will keep his resolution, but let him frequent the company of those who play, though at first only as a spectator, yet he will soon find his resolution fail. His imagination will flatter him with the hope of better success; the enticements of his companions to try his fortune again will bend him to compliance, or their derision and jeers will unman him.

How many instances are there of drunkards who, if kept entirely from liquor, will scarcely think of it. But let them go into company and take a glass or two, and they will not have resolution enough to restrain themselves from excess! A person may be honest and have even an abhorrence of all injustice, but let him be in difficulties, and have an opportunity of committing fraud with impunity, and who will answer for his honesty? Hence the common proverb that occasion makes the thief.

How many are there who of themselves would never think of speaking obscene words, yet if in company with those who talk in that strain, are carried away and speak as they do! From these and many such cases it is plain that the outward occasions of sin are the strongest means which the devil has of tempting us; his internal suggestions are frequently too weak and of no effect without the other, and he, well knowing this, does his utmost to lead people into dangerous occasions and to bring before their eyes the objects that excite to sin as the most effectual way to ruin them.

Thus, even with our blessed Savior Himself, after Satan had in vain tried to deceive Him by other means, "He took Him up into a very high mountain, and showed Him all the kingdoms of the world and the glory of them, and said, all these will I give Thee, if Thou wilt fall down and adore me" (Matt. 4:8). He could easily have told Him in the desert that he had all these kingdoms in his power and would give them, but he knew that presenting objects before the eyes makes a deeper impression and excites a more keen desire than anything that can be said in words. What he did then to Jesus Christ, he continues daily to do to men, and sad experience shows with what fatal success.

The sacred Scriptures declare the same truth and assure us how impossible it is for one to expose himself to these occasions and not be overcome by them. "Can a man hide fire in his bosom," says Solomon, "and his garments not burn? Or can he walk upon hot coals, and his feet not be burnt?" (Prov. 6:27–28). "He that touches pitch shall be defiled with it; and he that hath fellowship with the proud shall put on pride" (Ecclus. 13:1). Nay, the same Divine oracles declare that "he that loveth danger shall perish in it" (Ecclus. 3:27). How strongly is this confirmed by striking examples!

Dinah, the daughter of Jacob, passing through the country of Sichem, from curiosity, "went out to see the women of that country" (Gen. 34), and she met with dangerous company, lost her honor, and was ravished. David, by looking at a beautiful woman, though at a little distance, was hurried into two grievous sins, adultery and murder. Solomon with all his wisdom was not proof against the seduction of dangerous company; "He loved many strange women . . . and his heart was turned away by them to follow strange gods . . . and he worshipped idols" (3 Kgs 11:1, 4). Sampson with all his strength fell by the same means and lost both his liberty and life. Eve in her innocence, by listening to insinuating words, was seduced from her duty to commit a grievous sin, which brought ruin and misery on all her posterity. And St Peter, by dangerous company, was induced to deny his Master, and by oaths and imprecations to protest that he did not know Him! How dangerous, then, is it to expose one's self to the occasion of sin! "Evil communications corrupt good manners" (1 Cor. 15:33).

Hence we are commanded in the strongest manner to avoid all such occasions and to fly from them both by the law of nature, which strictly obliges everyone to avoid exposing himself to the danger of offending God and of ruining his own soul, and also by the express law of God, both in the Old and New Testament. Thus, when God forbade our first parents to eat of the fruit of the tree of knowledge, He at the same time forbade them so much as to touch it (Gen. 3:3), lest their touching it should prove an incitement to their eating of it.

So also, when He instituted the days of unleavened bread, He not only forbade His people to eat leavened bread during those days under pain of death but would not allow them even to have it in their houses, lest it should prove an occasion of their eating it. "Seven days," says He, "there shall not be found any leaven in your houses; he that shall eat leavened bread, his soul shall perish out of the assembly of Israel" (Ex. 12:19).

In like manner Almighty God, well knowing that the wicked inhabitants of the land of Canaan, if left among His people, would by bad example prove their ruin, prohibited them in the strictest manner from having any communication with them, or even from allowing them to dwell in the land, and thus He speaks: "I will deliver the inhabitants of the land into your hands, and will drive them out before you; thou shall not enter into league with them, nor with their gods; let them not dwell in thy land, lest perhaps they make thee sin against Me, if thou serve their gods, which undoubtedly will be a scandal to thee" (Ex. 23:31). "Beware thou never join in friendship with the inhabitants of that land, which may be thy ruin; but destroy their altars, break their statues, and cut down their groves. . . . Make no covenant with the men of these countries; lest when they have committed fornication with their gods, and have adored their idols, someone call thee to eat of the things sacrificed" (Ex. 34:12, 15).

"Neither shall thou make marriages with them. Thou shalt not give thy daughter to his son, nor take his daughter for thy son, for she will turn away thy son from following Me. . . . Their graven things thou shalt burn with fire; thou shalt not covet the silver and gold of which they are made, neither shalt thou take to thee anything thereof, lest thou offend, because it is an abomination to the Lord thy God. Neither shalt thou bring anything of the idol into thy house, lest thou become an anathema like it. Thou shalt detest it as dung, and shalt utterly abhor it as uncleanness and filth, because it is an anathema" (Deut. 7:3, 25). "Be not delighted," says Solomon, "in the paths of the wicked; neither let the way of evil men please thee. Flee from it; pass not by it; go aside and forsake it" (Prov. 4:14).

In the Gospel, our blessed Savior is particularly strong on this subject. "If thy right eye," says He, "cause thee to offend, pluck it out and cast it from thee; for it is better for thee that one of thy members should perish than that thy whole body should be cast into hell. And if thy right hand cause thee to offend, cut it off and cast it from thee; for it is better for thee that one of thy members should perish than that thy whole body should go to hell" (Matt. 5:29). Where observe that He does not say, if thy eye or thy hand be an occasion of sin to you, shut your eye, bind your hand, but pluck out thy eye, cut off thy hand. There is no dallying with these dangerous occasions, nothing but an entire separation can save us from perishing in hellfire; for "he that loves the danger shall perish in it" (Ecclus. 3:27).

No man must here trust to the strength of his own resolution, or expose himself to dangerous occasions, from the persuasion that he is firmly determined never to be led astray by them. However strong his resolution may be when at a distance from the occasion, what security can he have that he will not be unmanned when exposed to it? Is he stronger than Sampson, more pious than David, wiser than Solomon, or more faithful than Peter? They fell by being exposed to the occasions; what can he expect?

It is the argument of a fool to say, "At present, when I am in no danger, I am fully resolved not to commit the sin; therefore, when in the danger, and when the imagination is heated and the passions excited by its presence, my resolution will persevere in its full strength and vigor." "A wise man," says Scripture, "fears and declines from evil; the fool leaps over and is confident" (Prov. 14:16). This self-confidence was the principal cause of St. Peter's fall: "Though all should be scandalized in Thee," said he to his blessed Master, "yet will not I," and "though I should die with Thee, yet will I not deny Thee." He was not then in the occasion, but a little after when exposed to it, how shamefully did his courage fail him! How basely did he deny his Master!

Neither let anyone say that he trusts in the assistance of God, Who will preserve him. For though we may confidently trust that God will never fail to protect us in those dangers to which we are exposed in the course of duty, or which His Divine providence permits to come in our way, yet we have no reason to expect such protection when we voluntarily expose ourselves to the danger without a cause. Nay, such pretended confidence in God is nothing but presumption; it is therefore highly criminal. It is transgressing His express command to fly from the danger, to separate ourselves from it, though as dear as a hand or an eye, and is a provoking of Him to abandon us to ourselves in punishment of our folly.

So far is He from promising any assistance in such cases that He expressly declares, "He that loves danger shall perish in it." He does not merely say shall fall but positively assures us he shall perish in it. Where, then, are the grounds for hoping for assistance when, by exposing ourselves to the danger, we provoke His indignation and insult Him?

These, then, are the principal remedies against all the enemies of our souls, which, if we faithfully use the Divine assistance, will never be wanting to us, and the more diligent we are in doing our part, the more firmly may we hope for God's protection, and such an abundant supply of His grace as will enable us effectually to keep His holy commandments and attain eternal salvation.